OTHER BOOKS BY MICHAEL GUALTIERI

Declawing the Sphinx

Maledetti (The Forsaken)

About Michael Gualtieri

Michael Gualtieri is an Italian-born proud Canadian. He grew up playing baseball and finds soccer incomprehensible - a serious fault in an Italian. He is temperamental and volatile - a serious fault in a Canadian.

He confesses that nothing about his externalities is more than a random collection of events foisted upon him in his helplessness. He lives in a remote part of the Canadian Shield without television or a daily paper.

He has been cavalier enough to try his hand at many things including pioneering on a 500-acre homestead. This entailed endless physical work and risks - should you ever count the bugs of summer you will feel the risk.

The homestead remains untamed... perhaps if it had been 5 acres...but the need to build and repair persists. He has logged big and small trees and still has his limbs. He has built roads that beavers flooded away. He has raised a garden to provide abundance for the lazy moose and deer. He has entertained family and friends and they have not been pleased. Many of these tasks were actually done by his wife of 30 years, Frances.

None of these activities matter to him. "They are really just a noise," he complains. Only for his poetry does he stand, which he categorizes as "a few sparks in this all-too-long night".

Michael Gualtieri reiterates the sentiment of Francesco Petrarch , who states that, "You will find on that road small company, gentle spirit/therefore I pray and ask/do not desert your magnanimous task."

Canadian Carnival

Michael Gualtieri

St. Augustine Society Press
Reading Series

Published 2003
by St. Augustine Society Press
68 Kingsway Crescent
Toronto, Ont.
M8X 2R6
416-239-1670

Book design by Karen Terry Home and Business Services
705-645-9668

Canadian landscape art
McMichael Gallery, Kleinburg, Ontario
and other collections

Photographs of Japanese scenes
from various sources

Canadian Cataloguing in Publication Data
Gualtieri, Michael, 1947-
Canadian Carnival
(St. Augustine Society reading series)
Poems.
ISBN 0-9697157-3-0
I.Title. II.Series.
PS8563.U13C35 2003 C811'.54 C2003-901163-1
PR9199.3G788C35 2003

Printed and bound in Canada

Introduction

For a living soul to rise upon the promised land, much assistance is required. Many sadly falter since helping hands are indeed few. This gigantic transformation needs great labour. That which we must assemble is in size and number astonishing.

In my travels I have relied heavily on those of strength and dedication who came before. I stand with them absolutely. My progress is in large measure attributable to their great courage.

I set out to be clear and straightforward - eager to build a work on which I could depend, for nothing unsure, nothing impure will here endure. I have struggled to place secure signs pointing to the climb for all who "alone" must seek a way home.

All of my words are inadequate to the task of depicting the grandness of the transformation. My hope is that for those few near that the example suffices. Out of mysteries resolved it is possible to make a life.

Michael Gualtieri
Vankoughnet, Ontario
February, 2003

CONTENTS

Roughing it in Eden   1

Straightening the crooked road   57

Such a surprise, Paradise   109

Roughing it in Eden

Canada without snow

What is the point of crying,
do this to end the dying,
when I have no power.
Such is this poet's hour.

I can say over and over again,
they are all here,
this is the fate of man,
they shall always be here.

It cannot be, they say,
that all men are here today.
I insist that I am certain,
they call me impertinent.

Until you see as I
you'll continue to die.
For not accepting the truth
you'll be without root.

All men pass as shadows,
they cannot see the gallows,
and you wishing it not so
is a Canada without snow.

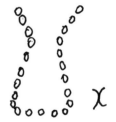

The Lord maketh poor and maketh rich.
He will keep the feet of his saints,
and the wicked shall be silent in darkness;
for by strength shall no man prevail.
                              I Samuel 2:7,9

A single grain of truth

Wouldn't it be great
if this piece started gracefully,
gradually revealing, easily unsealing.

Wouldn't it be great
if it did not offend
and there be no need for amends.

Then we might feel at ease,
comfortably pleased.

Let me ask: how would it feel if an officer
searched you head to toe
just because he wanted to know.

Yet we are so searched each living hour,
no, not for heroin or car stereos,
not for conjured plastic or the dollar majestic
but for one grain of truth.

Sadly it is rarely found,
for man weaves illusions
into a fabric of seamless confusion.

But for so long as planets spin
we'll be searched within,
and lest that grain be found
we'll keep to this boggy ground.

I the Lord search the heart.
I try the reins, to give to every man
according to his ways.
                    Jeremiah 17:10

Our spring full of storms

We measure one another by the fashions of the day,
some in silk and leather, some in polyester and suede.
We measure one another's muscle and are awed
or by pity startled when the wheelchair passes by.
We measure one another for the weight of coin
kept in the pocket next to the groin.

All of this measuring persistently gathered
adds up sadly to another day shattered.

Were we to look underneath the slyness
we would glimpse a scene electrifying.
Stunned, we could only stumble away
blinded, dazzled by the secrets inlaid.
Were we to look surely
we'd see the volcano devouring,
then we'd have our second beginning.
Were we to look purely
we would hear the screams hidden,
then we'd have our second beginning.

Then high and low would to their true good flow
for it is a dread unbearable, the ripping and tearing.
This is our spring full of storms,
the only escape from the gutting horn.

But your inward part
is full of ravening.
                    Luke 11:39

This desert

To go on
on in this desert
is a torture
grim and terrible
to be seared
burned
poisoned by scorpions
the earth boils
the sky cloudless
all man's bones are here
the flying heat
the harrowing sun
will I die here
snakes scurrying
barren
endless
gutting flames
will I die here
dried and died
a heap
I stand alone
unbearable
I see
sand eyes
crippled thought
better rats gnawing
than man's lying
and better this
all of this
than the land of denying.

Thou shalt thrice deny
that thou knowest me.

Luke 22:34

In circles you must go

Little one rising from the earth
humming with appetite for greater girth,
these needs that are formed
you'll find are a storm.
As a remedy I give this sealed chest
full of marvels, a help in your quest.
You'll be grown when again we meet
right here on this very short street.
It will be instantly clear, your state,
but I'll check if you've passed the gate.
Nearly all fail the unsealing -
nothing they do is redeeming.

Would it were not so,
in circles you must go.
In the world you appear a man dazzling,
here we see a tragedy passing.
You are a misery beyond repair -
the seal unbroken condemns you to the snare.

Therefore my people are gone
into captivity.
                                    Isaiah 5:13

They all, all hear

One sunshiny day walking in a tall green wood
I saw at the base of a gnarled white oak a titmouse
working.
I asked, can you, little fellow, hear me.
He certainly could, in a flurry of feet he swept away.

Nearby a thin, rust-tanned doe stood poking.
I wondered, could she hear me.
I called softly to her -
she turned in a flash and in strides Olympian stole away.

Next a fluffy, long-tailed fox in the undergrowth appeared.
Surely, I thought, this red fox can hear me.
I carefully made myself heard -
he paused, he looked, he sped away from the ground I stood.

Now I must say they all, all hear
and in hearing respond by fleeing.

The Islands of Despair

On the Islands of Despair
they do funny things there,
at least funny to me.
They scramble like lizards
up a stone wall.
They creep spasmodically
to ever higher ledges.
They hardly heed any rules
as they crash and smash,
unceasingly climbing.

Later when I come to look
they are where they've always been,
and the granite ridge is vibrating
from the cunning climbing.

These are others besides man
here on the Islands of Despair.
These are a charm
and know I can only say,
All of this climbing
is death delayed.

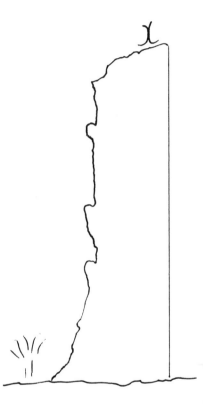

Come, behold the works of the Lord,
what desolation
he hath made in the earth.

Psalm 46:8

9

A child in the morning

Let us tell about a child in the morning
who gladly and eagerly, all seeking, all feeling
bounces off to teachers and classes and other things orderly.

She does not suspect and could not know
that all she will hear must later seem low,
nor that she is forced to accept
what later she must reject.

Today man is driven as a horse or a mule.
These are not by love ruled.
Rare is the teacher in peace abiding
and fewer in loving-kindness guiding.

Instead we have bad contrivances,
smiles concealing crying, confessions fully lying,
and many uniforms for our hiding.

Our needy child trapped in this concealing
is beguiled into continuing the deceiving.
This nine-to-five raising is grossly unfair
but seems to fill them with plenty of terror.

Be not as the horse
or as the mule
which have no understanding.
                    Psalm 32:9

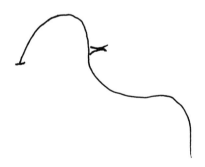

Merely his reflection

Blood my blood he drinks at every coming of thirst
blood my blood he drinks at every coming of thirst
blood my blood he gorges on
blood my blood he gorges on
and they sans a red corpuscle deny he exists.

Blood my blood this colossus drains
from my veins
he bleeds me canyon-dry
and they desert-dry laugh at me and deny.

I war for my blood
I war for my blood
flowing from my veins
and they who are merely his reflection
despise the misfit.

White Pine. *1957*
A.J. Casson

The city gate

In this day of scientism, of false erudition
not a one comprehends, not a bit,
these words of peace and glory
from the root straightforward.

It is sad and I've grieved plenty
over the wretchedness of this duplicitous dandy,
who rumbles and roars at every provocation
in the city full of people, the city full of noise.

I have ceased crying, 'would it were not so'
and accept calmly this noise confounding.
I stand humble and grateful at
the city gate hearing only the quiet.

It would be grand if they intended
to better separate from the rendering.

How doth the city
sit solitary
that was once full of people.

Lamentations 1:1

13

None dare escape

So large, so large, so very large,
none dare your size perceive.
Next to you Mount Trudeau is as an ant hill.

So loud, so loud, so very loud,
none dare your screaming perceive.
Next to you an explosion is as a cricket chirping.

So stormy, so stormy, so very stormy,
none dare your tumult confront.
Next to you a tsunami is as a lapping wave.

They are yours, none dare escape
while I keep on my side of the prison gate.

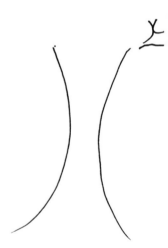

I will deliver thee
out of the hand of the wicked,
I will redeem thee
out of the hand of the terrible.
                    Jeremiah 15:21

He everywhere touches shadows

O tell me in my misery, what can a man perceive
if he is shoeless?
if he is learned?
if he is moneyed?
Let the answer come clearly to me
and I will record it faithfully.
Alas you say it could only be revealed
that he everywhere touches shadows
and does not know it.

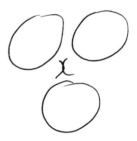

Shadows crushing

Know them as useless for heaven's sake;
stop kowtowing to these phantasms of illusion
for their deeds are evil; end your confusion.

Know them as utterly, totally useless save for business sake -
there they are, the anxiety that houses and educates,
feeds and medicates, perpetuating the slave state.

Know them wasted as did the others
for they hide in a mask by sorrow imbued;
to all of your steps, your very quickening, they are inured.

Know them ferociously, this justice demands
that sentence be passed and not equivocated
for they are the shadows crushing, in all ages.

Then see and feel as never before
the wonder, the magic of my open door.

And this is the condemnation, $))) (((\chi$
that light is come
into the world
and men loved darkness.
                    John 3:19

Out of the midst of fire

Into every ear, at a certain time of year
he whispers, "The cannon aimed at you is here."
By this easy stroke all are compelled
to firmly adhere to the magic of the spell.

He is not bashful and can be more unkind
but rarely does he remind, so obedient is mankind.
With his mastery over every man secured
to whisper more would just be absurd.

He whispers to make man conform
to the constant quiet before the storm.
By this brilliant stroke of ruining
we are spared much delicate doing.

For he who succumbs will labour
that bread and jewels adorn the table.

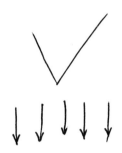

And upon earth he showed thee
his great fire
that thou hear his word
out of the midst of the fire.

Deuteronomy 4:36

Abandoned in the dark

Surely to place the blame on E.B. Eddy
or on hard-working Noranda Mines
is to misplace our furor.
Nor is sprawling Inco at fault
and Northern Telecom does not merit a dart.
This could be said of many a going concern
that they are not wastrels nor do they fail to learn.
Neither are our rulers to blame
for all of us who are so lame.
It is to the poets I point
for having missed the mark.
We remain abandoned in the dark.

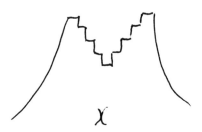

The signature of the day

Filled by the Noise
in their heads,
the absurd Noise
of non-being,
of man public,
they come together, this stony silence,
this silent heart,
the harvest of lies.

When they did reflect the Bible
it was never reconciled;
the Noise is just another confusion
in a long line of grand illusions.

I sense this will go on and on
for the choices made
are the same -
distractions make them lame.

Such is the signature of my day -
so very glad I got away.

For ye are dead, and your life
is hid
with Christ in God.

Colossians 3:3

The enemy with steady eye

Soldier, soldier deep in battle,
wild fire and ordinance dazzle,
zealous and feisty in deportment,
and at times thinking a sportsman.

This fickleness is by Me detested.
Some days you war relentless
and others you stop and dream
of dalliances, sunshine and streams.

But the enemy with steady eye
seeks each minute to brutalize.
When you are vigilant he retreats,
when you dream he is back on the street.

Then does this warrior pounce
until everything you renounce.
Submission to his will he desires,
thereafter nothing more will you require.

He contends with Me, this savage,
and leaves ghosts standing after the ravage.

See, I have set before thee
life and good
death and evil.

Deuteronomy 30:15

20

The members

Is there any place on earth
where men meet eye to eye, clearly,
where men meet heart to heart, purely.

Oh I know of men who lurking as
shadows, meet in their despair,
as members of the grand defeat.

Alas nowhere do men meet
without fear chaining their feet.

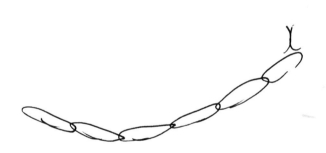

Let us embrace

Let us look for happiness
in a mask
that is fit on everyone
from mandarin to drunk.

Let us look for love
in a mask
which fits so tight
we wear it day and night.

Let us look for joy
in a mask,
the fate of the ape
in sad state.

Let us embrace and smile,
we've had this disease awhile.

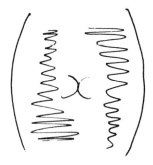

For I was envious at the foolish
when I saw the prosperity of the wicked.
For there are no bands in their death.
                    Psalm 73:3

Disguises

None dare see the massacre within
though all are able to look in.
Only one or two per generation
see man undisguised and naked.

Man driven, plays out games,
a chemical reaction briefly blazing.
So few rise, must be the low pay.
Does it matter, countless lost today?

Those whom the mysteries contact
are a progress unseen, unsuspected,
so successful is the destroyer
who never releases his quarry.

Yet upon the new land glorious
we unveil ourselves joyous.

God knoweth your hearts
for that which is highly esteemed among men
is abomination in the sight of God.
                              Luke 16:15

There they keep

If you would open up the door
he will be standing there
as he has for the past centuries
of forgotten lore.

If you would be bold and leave it open
he will, as is his wont, step right in.

He has no mask, no other task
but to heave and to batter, everything shatter
that is in you lazily gathered.

Be not frightened by this coming.
There is no avoiding him.
Be not frightened by this dismembering.
There is no avoiding him.

And as I look on every man
I am certain only the chosen
face these endless explosions.

The rest dwell in his victory.
They bristle to be sure.
But the invisible walls they do not breach
and there they keep in his easy reach.

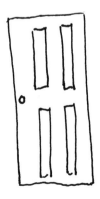

Obedient to commands

O fine man erudite,
such a bright satellite
running the show:
yes you, the CEO,
you the minister of state,
you on that nice estate
making decisions.

Decide well in your heart,
making love the greater part.

Too you must know
that good men like you
built Dachau
with all little hands
obedient to commands.

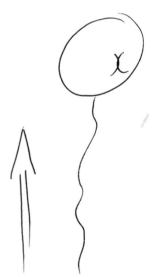

Love never faileth,
but where there are prophecies
they shall fail,
where there be tongues
they shall fail,
where there be knowledge
it shall fail.

Corinthians 13:8

The ticking of the clock

My friend, come in, come in.
I want to show you this thing
that is old and majestic.
Many times it has been resurrected
so that it will go on and on forever.

Hear it,
the ticking of the clock?
It does to me as to a leaf
and it knows not the difference.

Alas we are in its firm embrace
and surely as the pounding sea
or the ever-revealing sky of motion
this course it must run, poor me.

Nothing we can ever do
will hold back a tick or two.

This firm dread

O puffed-up man
you are such a scare -
your incomprehending ways,
a string of listless days.
Nothing you intend,
life you misspend.

Absolutely I am wary
of convictions so shallow.
Ever obedient to dictators.
Torturer of the courageous.
No matter how I try,
you I cannot set aside.

I have this firm dread,
so changeable are the dead.

And so marvel: for Satan himself
is transformed into an angel of light.
II Corinthians 11:14

Such a silence

I take away the tribal songs of teenage years.
I take away the country wailers shedding tears.
I take away the Madison Avenue prose of dues.
I take away the shabby academic clues.

I am left with silence. Such a silence!

Imagination once dark and forbidden is today
stolen outright by feeble men worn by delay.
Stolen and at once filled to the brim
with catchy phrases from the paralyzing din.

I am left with silence. Such a silence!

They who were once the echo of a single book
are this day smothered without even a look.
Under the droning of this dreary dread
they lie as if dead.

I am left with silence. Such a silence!

By the yellow lantern light a man was sold.
In these circumstances he could be brave, even bold.
This day the slaves are simply cored!

And I am left in such a silence!

But friend - do not sleep

In my day some have not enough to eat.
So it was yesterday when starving they died?
I fear for the many when tomorrow empty stomachs don't subside.

In my day some have not a place in from the cold.
So it was yesterday when they stopped and froze?
I fear for the many when tomorrow they find no abode.

In my day some ill receive no care.
So it was yesterday when untended they fell?
I fear for the many when tomorrow tolls an early knell.

My day straddles this fence of plenty and peril.
I pray let us move to disperse this giant shadow.
Then can man more easily come with me
and my thousand brothers
of the past ten thousand years
who escaped the hold of these desperate needs.

But friend - you there - do not sleep!
Be not deceived by your armour so deep.
For the enemy dismisses all of these distinctions
and visits upon you a sorrow permanent and piercing.

Lake Superior Island. 1923
Lawren Harris

Speak, though it may go unheard

A husky, tall man in the forest boreal
on the red granite of the Canadian Shield,
cruising for gold, finds Eldorado,
a ten-day trek out of Port Arthur.

Would you hear more of the gold he found,
the mother-lode beneath an inch of ground.
Would you have me reveal
how to great wealth unseal.

No one cares about the flies and bears,
the mosquitoes filling the air,
or the bones that do not mend,
for no-one is there to attend.

It seems clear that all is drear,
save the gold by the bold released from the hold.
All that is shiny and bright cascades
while the truth at first abrades.

How do we face this discouraging error,
for mighty discovery is fraught with terror.
If we do not speak clearly of the way,
no one will find any gold today.

Living Life, what am I to say to these astray.
What am I to do in these deceptions that rule.
"Speak, though it may go unheard :
only a man of sorrows escapes the herd."

The heart of the wise is in the house of mourning;
but the heart of fools is in the house of mirth.
                                        Ecclesiastes 7:4

Countless the shadows

Will you not see, not feel, not ever know
that they are intricate and fleeting as snow.
Will you not see, not feel, not ever know
that in a mask, task to task, they intensely flow.

Do you not see, not hear or ever sense
that they are a dreadful noise, a panic that does not end.
Do you not see, not hear, or ever sense
that they are today as the day Christ was sent.

Will you deny, all decry, and never feel
that the ways of man are brutal and mean.
Will you deny, all decry, and never feel
that man's nature is to connive and steal.

O come out of this pool vast,
for countless the shadows we must pass.

For what shall it profit a man,
if he shall gain the whole world
and lose his own soul?
                    Mark 8:36

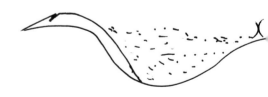

Endless is the drowning

Imagine this,
a man drowning
in a pool of poison
is offered a ready sop
saturated with poison.

Think this extreme?
Allow me to explain,
since you're on vacation.

This is the way of man everywhere -
that at an early stage of living,
the master brutal makes a call,
and thereafter the mould is set -
for endless is the drowning.

Disagree?
Think it otherwise?
I suspect you might.
But until you see as me,
it will be a very long night.

And the light shineth in darkness
and the darkness
comprehended it not.
                              John 1:5

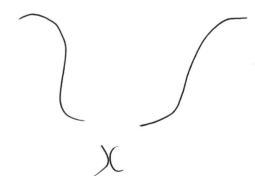

They are obedient

My Lord I feel afraid.
I am afraid of them forsaken
who are everlasting in the wailing.
They are obedient and are of the family
out of which they never tread
save to earn a piece of bread.

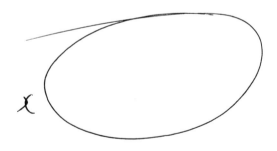

These are the reasons

Who has the heart
to suffer the loneliness
brought by the darkness.
The heart to keep the fire
casting shadows on the wall.
The heart to the giant battle
in the war which savages.
Who has the heart to grasp
the long march of masks.
The heart to overcome the conniving
of man's reckless striving.
The heart to measure the pace
of days passing in the race.
The heart to oneself keep
in fields full with sheep

and not surrender.

Few. And these are the reasons
men select treason.

Mark the perfect man
and behold the upright,
for the end of that man is peace.
                    Psalm 37:37

35

After the movie

After the movie
he went to his home
which was not much more than a room
to sit
and maybe read
about movies
which are about and only about
relationships
which do not exist.
Tomorrow he would
shop
and maybe catch another movie, then
after the movie...

The impenetrable mental curtain

When I was among the pygmies of New Guinea
in the roadless highlands of the Ramu River
or among the mudment of the Asaro Valley,
it was not possible to be uncertain
of the impenetrable mental curtain.

Now among them of Rosedale and Cabbagetown
near the border of the Canadian Exhibition grounds
or among the earners that Toronto surround,
it is not possible to be uncertain
of the impenetrable mental curtain.

Surprising how similarly they bend,
both severely fenced, only shallows tend,
marching through rituals and customs without end.
Marvellous how the Papuans only pose
and Yorkies only to lies are disposed.

I see by the grace of the living light
that both rise and it is always night.

When all workers of iniquity do flourish,
it is that they shall be destroyed forever.
                    Psalm 92:7

37

So near the crowning room

O mighty man
who these words
dismiss
as ramblings idle.
Why do you not see
all that you build
is infamy?

So many doomed,
so near
the crowning room.

Sadly the key to the prison door
is unseen
though it has just fallen
on the floor.

Listen well my friend

If a man should elect not to war
here in this nationless promised land,
he will, be sure, nevermore stand.

If a man seeks from the war to hide
here in this landscape of eyes,
the enemy will uncover and pulverize.

If a man seeks to escape the war
to the Lesser Antilles at Montserrat,
the magma there will erupt and blast.

So, little human, little man,
war is waged wherever you land,
so fierce, so long, his dread hand.

Listen well, my friend, and battle
or be herded with the cattle.

For he is not a man,
as I am,
that I should answer him,
and we should come together in judgement.
                    Job 9:32

Fully his are them of the mask

Fully his are them of the mask.
I write on my skin
with this sharp glass
that he who enters to tear all away
can never remove these words impressed
into the fabric of my bare chest.

Fully his are them of the mask
and not for six days excluding Sunday
but every minute of every breathing hour
he surely devours
keeping them supine.
Not one escapes his power.

Fully his are them of the mask.
None deny him his victory.
None enter the great mysteries.
Nor have any arrived
in the second child,
by the light that I abide.

Fully his are them of the mask.
I have come to this hard knowledge
that nothing will dislodge them
from his grasp.
So in the parade I lift high my feet
and in peace my happiness keep.

Since the beginning of the world

I wake in my little room
in Kingston, Toronto or Kapuskasing
alone, save for the other -
always waiting is this brother.

Each day he is there
by my bed in his lair,
scheming to make me dead,
the only quest of this dread.

Would he were a thief looking to steal
or a gangster wishing to deal.
His one desire is my tormenting
over and over unrelenting.

When the deed is complete
sealed is my defeat.
He makes me full of rage,
my blood on every page.

He fits on me a mask
of exquisite construction
concealing the self-hatred
and the self-destruction.

Thus I lose the war -
would it were a metaphor.

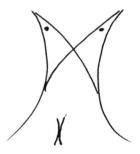

For since the beginning of the world
men have not heard,
nor perceived by the ear,
neither hath the eye seen.

                    Isaiah 64:4

Princely power

Hear the trumpet anthem
calling
as it has for a thousand years
you to arms
for the nation.

But never have you heeded the
call
to war
against the enemy
who in his princely power
walketh in to devour.

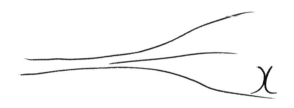

Time to stop and look

O little man made a king or queen
on this Eden pasture green,

dupe of the ruler unseen,
dupe of title, of position,
man concealing perdition.

O little man that Cadillac driving
down the highway gliding,
dupe of the ruler hiding,
dupe of gloss,
man tossed.

O little man covered by gold and silver
and friends that deliver,
dupe of the master bitter,
dupe of smiles,
man vile.

O little man being entertained
by dancers and elephants tamed,
dupe of him who lames,
dupe of the dizzying stage,
man always on the same page.

O little man absorbing the news
forming your views,
dupe of the ruler amused,
dupe of the babble,
man, just like cattle.

It is time to stop and look -
better had you written another book.

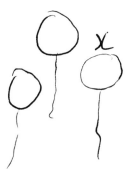

That they may recover themselves out of the snare
of the devil,
who are taken captive by him
at his will.

2 Timothy 2:26

North Town: Biscotasing. *1927*
Franklin Carmichael

I could tell them about the games

When from my window I scan the city scene
I want to pack my things and leave
for my country cabin in the high woods
there to hear, to surely feel
and become clear on the patchwork city quilt.

I now am certain that the crowds looking in shops
or hurrying off to earnings and raising little ones,
are not so different from them of past ages.
I can leave them here
for their obedience to appearance
is a monolith tall, an impenetrable wall.
On my return they'll still be there looking
at the wide mirror which is not working.

I could tell them about the games
but alas they are so intensely playing
that I leave them in the slaying.

Cycle of ages

Where there is one chickadee you will find two
and where a bluejay will be, a few.
They seek together within a near measure,
and that which they uncover is their treasure.

Though they know not the other's name,
they fight and flash, intense in every game.
A marvel of like appearance, in a clan keeping,
all others they spurn upon meeting.

With the opening of spring they sing
to charm and little ones bring,
whom they raise with great dedication,
pride and fabric of the nation.

To nature's baton they orchestrate,
ever secure in their estate;
for nothing do they suspect or doubt -
after all, they do not choose the route.

After the raising they move on to other parts:
such is the tempo and majesty of nature's art.
This cycle of ages we do not disrupt
for in it we anxiously play our part.

Consider the lilies how they grow -
they toil not and spin not.
Yet Solomon in all his glory
was not arrayed like one of these.
                              Luke 12:27

That side of the farm gate

This day of mine there is no escaping
the fool and his endless debating.
Also I am saddened when I look
at them caught on ambition's hook.

He who until yesterday would in a village be staying
is today in the tube smiling and braying.
And they who once plotted stealing and dealing
are at the club their dreary fate sealing.

They conceive only to deceive and no-one is exempt
from these machinations so worthy of our contempt.

I am sure that were they in my grasp I'd not err
but cash them in for a quieter air.
Alas I dream. It is not to be,
not now, not for eternity.
And not again should I expect other
on that side of the farm gate eating fodder.

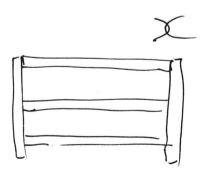

One clear, honest word

- *And now you shall receive*
  final judgement of all your years.

- *I'd rather not hear this*
  but likely you will insist.

- *It is for many a surprise,*
  this harvest of a life of lies.

- *I am hesitant to tell*
  for this is the final bell.

- *You do not seem too eager to know -*
  into fantasies you'd rather go.

- *I've lived always in noise,*
  my state of impoverished choice.

- *A life not having heard*
  one clear, honest word.

- *For judgement is given every day,*
  every moment, in every way.

- *I'm starting to see my state,*
  standing near this heavy gate.

- *Nothing in you can be concealed,*
  to us all is open and revealed.

- *Everything I did deny;*
  to you I closed my eyes.

- *It seems I've been deceived*
  and final judgement is received.

For nothing is secret;
neither shall anything be hid
That shall not be revealed.
                    Luke 8:17

Here they blissfully keep

God's creatures nearly countless
and in variety virtually endless
do not on any day
give a thought to tomorrow
or to yesterday.

They do not at all despise
the man with the scythe
or fear the unforgiving sweeping
this huge pendulum is keeping -
no, not even to a small degree.

How different I am makes me wary
for the distance is so much greater
than one could expect to generate
by looking at the skin or the organs within.
Certainly the winter wind is to us indifferent
and many diseases equally come visiting.

But mine enemy they cannot know
nor reach the land of untouched snow.
So here they blissfully keep
removed a bit from sleep.

A concealed disaster

My dog with firm finality decides
while I in a flood of doubts abide.
For this we are each rewarded -
she hears no doubt, I am seriously routed.

Many think it obvious and clear
that men stand certain without any fear.
Yet I have found that as I travel,
uncertainties are as numerous as gravel.

It appears I stop the light
but I am a shadow full of fright.
It appears that I transact well
while I am fleeing the ringside bell.

It is not possible to explain
or make this chasm plain,
for when he of all illusion is master,
we become a concealed disaster.

Is it nothing to you,
all of you that pass by?
Behold and see if there be
any sorrow like unto my sorrow.

Lamentations 1:12

By the sea

I walk, he walks, we walk
in him.
I hear, he listens, we hear
in him.
I speak, he shouts, we speak
in him.
I feel, he feels, we feel
in him.
I see, he perceives, we see
in him.
These he does to me
as is the land covered by the sea.

The countless

Imagine as Epimenides did
that we are condemned to a life full of lies.
Then may we hear the lies he speaks.
It is a mighty surprise to find
that he turns all into lies.
That which is clear he churns to mystify.
Look as we might there is no escaping him.
We are able to rise or are doomed to sighs.
Everywhere around us the noises of man are a din,
the payment for co-operating with him.
Their days are full of this dreadful drone.
In the nights they grasp at his horrid throne.
Thus is the eternal will fulfilled
that man is to justice driven and not killed.

By his lies he breeds. Nothing more does he need.
Only lies does he tell to drive the countless into hell.

None are exempt

If I could keep my eyes
from mine enemy
who steals,
I'd behold the endless fields
of listlessness,
I'd sense the determination
concealing agitation,
I'd know them in the dark
fleeing every spark.

If I could my eyes keep
from mine enemy
who deceives,
I'd hear the denying
and bloody conniving,
for none are exempt
from the laws by heaven sent.

It would be a joy to these keep
as my signposts to every sad street.

It is not reason
that we should leave the word of God,
and serve tables.
                                        Acts 6:2

They are subdued

None see thee!
It's outrageous,
this way of ages.

To a few it's a hearty laugh
how generations fail to grasp
that though you are Mount McKinley size,
you completely deceive their eyes.

You are right here
seeing
them low, them beaming.

Should you spot any agitation
towards the master of sensation,
a piercing scream ensues
and at once they are subdued,
convinced easily once more
that Mount McKinley is way off-shore.

Terrors take hold on them as waters;
a tempest stealeth them away in the night.
                              Job 27:20

He does not sigh

It comes, it comes,
no place to run.
It comes to every man,
this final judgement grand.

It comes complete,
discrete,
surprisingly neat.

It comes, it comes,
our only fun,
sure as the sun.

None of the weak does he keep,
driving them into the pit deep.
For them high he does not sigh,
joining them with the small fry.

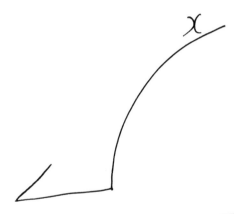

Only a few can this discern.
From the new land we see them burn.

For whosoever hath,
much shall be given;
whosoever hath not,
from him shall be taken away.
                    Matthew 13:12

Straightening the crooked road

Here starts the fighting

If I could ask Supreme Commander Eisenhower
or General Rommel of the Axis power
about mine enemy, about the war,
I would not be shocked to hear
that mine enemy they do not know.
As to how this giant I am to battle,
they suggest that a council be gathered.

If I could ask white-coated Carl Gustav
or Sigmund Freud, colleagues of similar parts,
about mine enemy, about the war,
I would not be shocked to hear
that they only bandage
the light wounds of battle,
that indeed they are committed to healing
but the prisoner - smiling -
must keep tight the bindings.

On and on and on this goes.
No one a help.
This certainly is disquieting,
for here starts the fighting,
and mine enemy does not wait,
and soon arrives a new date.

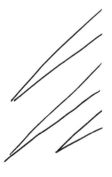

Be vigilant, for the enemy,
as a roaring lion, seeks to devour.
                    I Peter 5:8

Born to ride the sea

To read one single, solitary line of the Good Book
and apprehend
we must be as a surfer riding a ten-storey wave.
Surely on the edge of this surf the ride is thrilling,
each nerve on fire for suddenly can come a killling.

Look keenly to avoid the sharp-shinned shoals.
Here the sea is everywhere full of opinions, causes
and their senseless espousers.

Look keenly to avoid the dead-head logs furiously bobbing.
Here the sea is everywhere full of priests beguiling
and their sheep subscribing.

Any of these could do the killing.

We are born to ride the sea to land
and in our own bounty, happy stand.

Forever in the earth

I am not as them mesmerized by the easy fact
that colliding continents push up mountains
or that the moon and earth are caught in a weighty dance
or that unseen atoms can be divided.
But by this cadaver which yesterday I placed in the cold soil
I am ensnared for he is now sitting, grinning across my desk.
His icy look sends me reeling, fearing.
There is nothing else for me to do but labour mightily and nail
him once more into that pine box near to the railing.
But in this land of denial, he'll demand a retrial.
He will not stay, hence tomorrow will be as today.
He will enter, this dread, into my heart
unlike the tricky workings of the universe which have a smaller part.
He compels me and I must turn to face the horror
wherein I am to fulfil the vow of my birth
that I unsparingly labour until he is forever in the earth.

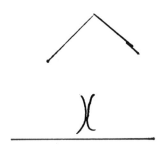

My one hope

Why don't I pretend that I have a friend?
Why don't I pretend that I have money?
Why don't I pretend that I have family?

For! I have come this way accompanied.
I have come this way spending easily.
I have come this way in a family.

Yet! I confess that the table is set for one.
Confess that I cannot pay and get out of here.
Confess that I am spurned by my family.

For! I cannot, as other men, pretend to have a friend.
I cannot, as other men, pretend to cherish gold.
I cannot, as other men, hide in a family.

But! Most of all I'll not pretend not to see the mask.
Pretend not to see the darkness in which men pass.
Pretend not to hear the screams they are concealing.

Now! My one hope is that my rising not fail.
For! Pretending in the gross darkness is of no avail.

For, behold, the darkness shall
cover the earth,
and a gross darkness the people.
                              Isaiah 60:2

A fine castle

When I speak of the gold I found I hear my
coarse, rough voice and would that I were sounding more
like the bubbling of a cascading stream or
the elegant calling of a dove so that your
fine hearing would find it pleasing.

The workings of my mind forming
images of the light are also coarse and rough.
It does not flow lucidly or directly
but rather circuitously and fragmentedly.
I would rather have you sense the pulsing of a zooming jet,
instead I confess a glider by the turbulence upset.

Neither does my pen on paper scribe
what I am able to design.
It is inevitable and I must accept
that no man's hand can render clear
that which is most free.
Yet with the finest steel that the smithy annealed
I construct a hint of the grand glory
that men have discerned for all of us.
Should you ever glimpse the stair,
thrust on and build with me, a fine castle in the air.

Out the prison door

Having lived many days
I have no more to read
or any voice which to heed.
Now I am to read myself
and rise from the depths.
I'll need to sit here a bit
until my pieces securely fit.

Duplicitous man is of no aid
and I'll not decry this difficult way
for my labour gains the reward -
I am now out the prison door.

Come, meet thy jailor towering,
surely you know his conniving.
There can be no doubt
that he fills you with his shouts.

These shouts that do not wake
imprison you in his rough estate.

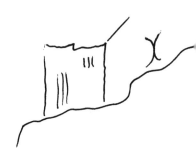

To open the blind eyes,
to bring out the prisoners from the prison,
and them that sit in darkness
out of the prison house.
                    Isaiah 42:7

Running free

From the peak of Kilimanjaro I did leap
(in the hope, my soul to keep)
on to a passing cloud, chased by him of scorn,
that Behemoth eternal of the piercing horn.

No, no, he yelled at me, do not flee!
It is unseemly, escaping from me.
Come, come! Stay as you have been,
settled in my arms, from rim to rim.

No, no, I yelled back, running free.
Never! Will I again return to thee.
No, no, this will not stand,
you belong here in my hand.

No, no, I'll no more be jailed
in the prison of them failed.
No, no, you must return,
no one escapes my churn.

No, no, that is a lie,
my brothers passed by.
But, hey. You know this very well,
it is your way of keeping us in hell.

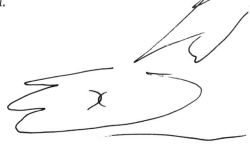

There is hope

Why must it all be so obscure to men
who have more than just a passing chance
to discern the difference between the fire and its shadow.
It doesn't seem fair that so many are locked
into their uncomprehending ways forever
who could have alighted and travelled on.
Alas I think it so - poor teachers add to woe.
It is the wine of error drunk to us by intoxicated teachers.
Also the poets frightened by the busy air tumble down the stair.
Yet all is not doomed to defeat eternally
since the record is there to be seen
and a few still scrawl beyond compare.
For them bold, them that dare
there is hope of climbing, though the sight be rare.

A *new footprint*

What is the merit of my stringing,
cobbling these words together
when others do it far better?
What is the merit of delicately
gathering, precisely tending,
when others do it far better?

It is that I am compelled.
I must crawl where others fly,
labour mightily where others glide.
This to end the subterfuge,
the gross dismemberment,
the frightening deluge.

I step only on the well-marked way.
Without these footprints to follow
I would be lost as any other.
My desire is to honour the explorers
who this twisting road uncovered,
for the essences desired this way are discovered.

May I continue this high task dedicated
and add a new footprint to the ages
that more may follow into salvation.

And after the earthquake
a fire;
but the Lord was not in the fire:
and after the fire
a still small voice.

                    1 Kings 19:12

Frood Lake. *1939*
Franklin Carmichael

Look

*Look to the centre of your being - here amidst distraction upon distraction,
noise upon noise, falseness upon falseness, you will glimpse it
fleetingly and run away in fear.*

*Look to the centre of your being - with all of your courage and hope, with
all of your strength and dedication, begin the labour of years, begin
the hard effort that leads to purity.*

*Look to the centre of your being - amidst the mysteries and magic, among
the most hidden of secrets there is our source, barely seeable, ever so
fragile - the power of powers, the end of all our dreams.*

*Look to the centre of your being night and day. Rest not. Look with every
ounce of energy and slowly, as spring emerging in Canada, barely
perceived, a flower rises from the earth. New beauty and wonder
come to life.*

This glorious morn

Hovering over planet, two extraterrestrials

- *Look, let's get down to business, we must be clear
  and report that there is no consciousness on this blue sphere.*
- *Shall we look elsewhere then, at another planet?*
- *I hate to appear hasty, but all that I discern on my screen
  is energy conformed to a mask.*
- *But as we, they hold the text of gold.*
- *That is why I am breathlessly surprised.*
- *At least in time past some walked here.*
- *It may once have been, as is recorded, one in a thousand.
  Now it is sadly less. Look, some appear.*
- *Shall we report one in a million?*
- *We would, it seems, be there when we measure
  one in a hundred million survive the storm
  And walk clear upon the earth on this glorious morn.*

Come to land

Sometimes I think it's hopeless -
after all, we've had this talk
about the shadows on the wall
so many times
over the past three thousand years.

I really would like to give up on you
as by now you're surely inured
to my beseeching.
Yet despite all of this
I want to believe
that soon you will be hearing.

Still it is a grinding this binding on the threshing-room floor
and it is not easy gleaning in this bitter wind that is streaming.

I shall keep to my vows, I'll not be remiss.
To any hand reaching from the lip of the abyss,
I'll lend mine, and one or two I'm sure
will come to land forever away from the endless lures.

He will retreat

It is such a hidden, secret place,
full of mysteries and in the end, grace,
full of secrets in the end unsealed,
full of wounds in the end healed.

The ruling monolith we see, we measure,
for we must deprive him of his treasure.
I am awed to see that we are able
to displace him from the head of the table.

From our presence he will retreat
though never very far from our feet.
It is between us that all will be resolved,
with a little help and our steadfast guide.

There is no greater labour to be done
than to battle here and end his long run.

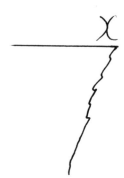

Mine eyes shall see
my desire
upon mine enemy.

                    Psalm 92:11

Flashes in the night

My friend struggling to be true
to me and to yourself
I can this say to brighten your eyes -
then you may rest well and feel sure
for there is no higher, nothing mightier.

Men are blinded by flashes in the night
and thereafter live every day hiding away.
Now and then they'll peek around
and a distant thunder hints and pounds.

They cannot the pit discern
for their master denies and burns
and with eyes wide shut
they are condemned to strut.

Nor can they see the others
that crowd in the roiling
for their master compels them to believe
that they alone have fallen.

Now, my friend true,
raise your master new
as I have
then peace and joy gather.

This is my comfort
in my affliction
for thy word
hath quickened me.
                    Psalm 119:50

Life will be just fine

On the day that I was born
a gentle angel in high Orion
full of hope in the abundance of birth's healing
placed a light in a lamp with kind feeling.

Today some fifty years have gone by -
all I've done is search low and high
but the lamp's switch I've failed to espy.

But I pray, pretty angel, stay,
don't take that lamp away.
I'm looking hard as I can -
surely soon I'll find the hidden man,
then that light will surely shine
and my brief life will be just fine.

I seek only my salvation

I seek only my salvation -
not to replace the high of no resolution
as in the October revolution.

I seek only my salvation -
not to entreat the powers political
to abandon their position so regal.

I seek only my salvation -
not to lessen the squabbling
of scholars and lawyers cunning.

I seek only my salvation -
not to lessen the noise deafening
upon all our hopes crashing.

I seek my salvation sure -
for nothing else will endure.

This is the day which the Lord hath made,
we will rejoice and be glad in it.
Psalm 118:24

Released from the shackles

Why do I not simply rest
and hear him
and see him tethered
and quiet.

Why do I not simply rest,
knowing that the darkness is cast-iron set.
Nothing will move them away from him,
nothing on earth could release them
from his shackles.

Why do I not simply rest
and nurture my child
and in this beauty serene
let my living heart feel
the free man released from the shackles.

The family storm

How could the mother tormented, raise the child to love
and the father labouring brutalized, be a sea of calm,
and both in a wide reign of wild expectations domiciled
breed illusions fantastic in a high-walled pride.

Let us no longer heed the perpetuated mad spell
that they who raised us were moved by a grand cause
when it was really a cloud of impenetrable disguises
that formed in us a very sad place in which we hide.

Let us cast away this litter from the family storm
that in us is intricately arrayed and always worn
for it leads us astray in a stream of lost days
that generation after generation is a callous delay.

Step by step we can reverse the harm
that our child be weighted down by lighter charms.

And thou shalt eat the fruit
of thine own body,
the flesh
of thy sons and of thy daughters.
                    Deuteronomy 28:53

77

I made silence

It was you, my friend, as we strolled around
who pointed him out hovering close to the ground.
I shunned to see him then for by the colours bright
and all of the gay faces in the light
he appeared translucent grey, even opaque to my sight.
I should have looked better for it is a rare matter
to see the enemy of man among those he scatters.

It was he who blinded me on that first day
as I started on my way.
It seemed impossible to do and it took ages
in that rank cavern
to regain my sight.
I should have been wary of him from the start.
His yelling pierced my hearing
until there was only the screaming - it echoed hard
in that rank cavern
until with all of my strength I made silence.

It was you, my friend, who first pulled at his claw
deep in me.
For this sole deed I am true.
In my heart I keep you.

78

Life precious

We are but a single strand of thread
which in a moment fails and snaps.
Struggles end in this final gasp,
for those who hunger and those overly fed.

What is the good of man's endeavours?
Does the worrying, the climbing matter?
We are so vulnerable,
and live ungovernable.

Before life stops, hear The Noise, the constant clamour.
See the sleepwalkers who gather and chatter.
This Noise, this chatter is of no merit.
Man's motions, a dreadful, crippling habit.

Let life precious not pass in vain;
join us who battle to all things gain.

I say that an untimely birth is better than he,
for he cometh in with vanity,
and departeth in darkness.
                              Ecclesiastes 6:3,4

Let echo into all homes

Hear, O hear, dark and dangerous one.
Hear a word from this bloodied throat.
Hear me, angel of doom, and despair my one word. Forever!

Forever I will crawl when I cannot walk.
Forever into this battle my life I place.
Then can the wailing be behind
and the pit's screams stilled.

Forever I must have my desire on you -
that I keep you silent.
Hear, O hear, let echo into all homes:
Forever from this storm man is born.

The thorny nest

On a green isle in mid-Atlantic
between dark Africa and wide America
two princes of the realm did contend
to make man to their rule bend.

Before the King they swore not to war
against any beast, nation or each other.
They were to seek man's domination.
Thus was set in motion our salvation.

As long as man kept night and day
hunting and harvesting away,
the princes would keep at bay,
heeding the edict recently laid.

These princes were different as land and water.
One was peaceful, the other full of fire.
When man dared take his first step
he was easily snared into a thorny nest.

This is the way it is, little one, reaching out.
There are two princes, one does not shout.

The heart of the sons of men is full of evil,
and madness is in their heart while they live,
and after that they go to the dead.
                              Ecclesiastes 9:3

Though I tremble

My friend, come and attest
that mine enemy who knows no rest
I must tame or forever be lame.

My friend, as you told me in the storm,
it is impossible to bend him with the horn
by showing him any university degrees.
Neither can he be made to obey
by any amount of money at his feet laid.
Nor will he bow in a palace ornate
or lessen his glance in a hovel of disgrace.

My friend, you who led him by a thread,
help my hand which by this rope of silver and gold
must this colossus place in a secure hold.
I am afraid. This halter is paper-thin,
a feather could unleash him.
Yet I lead him to a place of quiet
that he cease to smite at the end of night.

In trust of you, my friend,
I keep silent this Komodo dragon.
Though I tremble as I do,
I am certain you tamed him too.

This planet of leases

Here I am, my good Lord
in the noise deafening,
my feet on mines threatening.
Sad masks I behold
beneath many smiles cold.
Such is this day my sorrow,
my pain, my horror.

Unable to rise
I will not compromise.
My shattered limbs
I compel to swim.
Blind, I reach to feel.
Torn, I claw to reveal.

This is my way of peace
on this planet of leases.
Eye to eye I meet their cause
then no more myself despise.

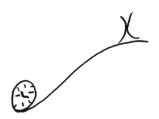

O ye sons of men,
how long will ye turn my glory into shame?
How long will ye love vanity, and seek after leasing?
Psalm 4:2

Northern Lake. *1923*
Lawren Harris

A man must rise

Somewhere a man must rise,
for what are we
when in toil
we live and die.

Somewhere a man must rise,
for we are not as
the many think,
that which we eat in.

Somewhere a man must rise
and slumber no more
for sunset nears
and to the darkness there is no end.

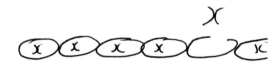

Make an end of this dust to dust

Certainly, certainly I feel his lash rip my back
until my bones, my nerves he does expose,
then the flash of his whip becomes a frenzied blur.

He does not pause, no never.
His dreaded poisons flow like Niagara.
Beatings upon beatings tear away my face.
This he does to the best of the race.
Not in the day, not in the night does his aim err.
My blood-choked screams fill the air.

Lord, is there an end of terror?

His beatings will stop
when I do as I must
and make an end of this dust to dust
by placing my feet on the rock of trust.

The rough road

My good companion loving and constant,
I have too much tripped and stumbled,
and always you did hope and care
that I no more fall down the stair.

The choices I made were full of error,
to distractions falling, my life a terror.
On this rough road I was torn and tossed,
such were my days among them lost.

This was the just reward and hard
which you my friend sought to discard.
You looked to release me from the sorrow,
never sparing, for there is no tomorrow.

It was dreadful, my poor choosing,
all of the suffering, everything losing.
Yet in all of these gambits sad,
for your constant love I am glad.

I will be with thee,
I will not fail thee,
nor forsake thee.
                    Joshua 1:5

87

Shield me from him

I wonder
what manner of man
could stand in this storm where I am bowed and torn?
Over and over I've been defeated
by the enemy herein secreted.
Year after year this battle I've waged
and this day still I am eaten by rage.

Lord on high, this is the grand design
wherein man's glory is just illusion
which he preserves to their endless confusion.
I bow to you, mighty one,
you keep them on a steady run.

Lord, enter upon my sad refrain,
help me my eyes and ears to gain.
Shield me from him who maims.

The issues of life

My Lord I am so afraid
that my reader
will become ashamed
reading your name.
And they who read on
will suddenly stop at one word wrong.

It is so sad
that all whom I see
for a word stop and preen.
They cannot the whole grasp
and then are lost,
confounded and tossed.

Would they knew humility
and glimpsed the hatred
of which they are sated.

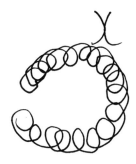

Keep thy heart with all
diligence
for out of it are the issues
of life.

Proverbs 4:23

Then in peace my soul I'd keep

My candle, Lord, is steadily burning away,
soon it will reach its natural end of day.
All the while that it has been lit, the darkness
has not receded, no, not one bit.

Clouds of fear swirl in my head.
Voices proclaiming, fill me with dread.

In my sparse light, on this stormy night,
Lord I beseech thee, help me to stay
this blackness that keeps me so frail
in screams of denial, all doubting.
I cannot go on in this darkness tormenting,
help me to end the horror unrelenting.

If I were certain that my little candle
could this hovering shadow dispel,
then in peace my soul I'd keep.
Good Lord come, guide my feet.

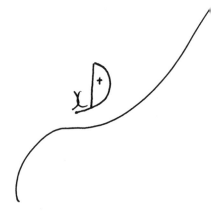

It can end

And death came upon everyone,
death, death, death, death
relentless,
knocking on every door.

Can I be released
from this swooning,
sweeping,
I'd like to know,
it is so grim where I go.

They are firm in their way,
not distinguishing night from day.
Such a dread sight,
this never-ending blight.

Can I be released
out of the sorrow,
out of this stark rock
that the prince keeps dark.

It can be.
It can be different tomorrow.
It can end, this sorrow.

Then I
will feel free
in peace and near to thee.

To rebuild is vital

In today's scheme of measures
I have mostly found pillaged treasure,
so I'd better be clear, the United States Army is grand,
and my Catholic Church a sad one-night stand.
Now I am to carefully place them side by side
to better discern and finally decide.

I see the United States Army as ordered and capable;
the lowest it raises until they are able
to Shermans and missiles assemble and use,
for they learn and achieve, and nothing confuse.
Recruits disparate become dedicated and loyal,
steadfastly embracing their perilous toil.

Not like this is my Roman Catholic Church
which has always left me in a lurch.
It is a failing, nowhere sailing,
a paralysis of endless ailing.
It seems late but to rebuild is vital
that we finally receive our high title.

For ye are like a whited sepulchre
which appears beautiful
but within
is full of uncleanness.
                    Matthew 23:27

I am made to overcome

This day I pray, as did Laocoon
that not a single cell invade my body
and then outrageously multiply.

This day the branch of a tree might
enter as Neoptolmus in the Trojan Horse
and crush my home and all inside.

This day a dragon of no remorse
could my wife and daughter
in a moment devour.

Are there terrors greater than these?

O driven soul truthfully utter:

Yes, there is a torment harder.

In this infinite realm of darkness
it is the enemy at my side
who alone condemns me to the ebb tide.

It is him I am made to overcome
as a diver the distance to air.
It is him I am made to overcome
as a man taming the possible terrors.
It is him I am made to overcome
or be no end of errors.

So hidden is our demise

I am free in this Nechako River valley,
free to choose where to travel,
coast downstream to hazy Prince George
or against the current escape this gorge.

In this barren BC wilderness I am to select,
or others will, between my life or my death.
I can paddle or cast the paddle aside -
this decides where I shall abide.

O I could join a wolf pack
and prowl proudly, everything sack.
I could there hide my lies
especially from my own eyes.

Here I could raise a shelter grand
or doze as others on the shifting sand.
My canoe in this wild river is racing -
it will be my salvation or decimation.

No one will know should I not survive,
for so hidden, so unseen is our demise.

I delivered the poor that cried,
and the fatherless,
and him that had none to help him.
                                    Job 29:12

I am as a feather

Mine enemy I behold

I am here seeking freedom

I bow to you my prince

There is no end to his jail

I am as a feather

To me you are alarming
I long for the calming

The Ice House. 1923
Lawren Harris

Giants only reach

We call out clear and no one does hear.
We seek the hiding and they remain there abiding.
We speak to all and only echoes call.

Why is this road so difficult and steep?
Why do so few the peak reach?
Perhaps you did not well teach?

A thousand million minnows in a school
fly from a spark for in them is completely dark.
This is the lot of them that become easily lost.

Like Niagara dashing men downward are crashing
though everyone is certain they are rising
with the movie stars they are aspiring.

Giants only, reach this new land
whose road never can be altered
despite the countless that fail and falter.

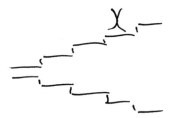

Thou wilt show me the path of life:
in thy presence is fulness of joy.
Psalm 16:11

Enter little prince

So many dead.
Help me little prince,
my redeemer given.

So many dead.
Release me from this hold
that I grow no more old.

So many dead.
They fill me full of screams
from mine enemy reaping.

So many dead.
Help me escape
this closing gate.

So many dead.
Enter, little prince, and raise
that I step happily my few days.

For to be carnally minded is death,
but to be spiritually minded
is life and peace.
                              Romans 8:6

Indeed it would be rare

Imagine a railroad from here to there
if you care
with now and then a missing span -
certainly it wouldn't be worth a damn.

Similarly here in this thin air:
a little gap in space
and we fall back into the race.

So everything we check
and check again as never before
to avoid being thrown out the door.

And when we err there is no avoiding
the collision that is boiling.
For to everything there is a price -
now isn't that nice.

My friend, be vigilant, beware
classifying molybdenum as barium,
for a beating will ensue
and it will crush you.

Indeed it would be rare
but should you build with care,
you will rise ever slow
as they slide there below.

Away, away, away, far away

Let my eyes look in
away, away, away, far away
from them who belong to him.

Let my eyes to my heart look in
away, away, away, far away
from them who belong to him.

Let my eyes to the mighty mystery look in
away, away, away, far away
from them who belong to him.

Let me accomplish this warrior feat,
then in my new-potent will the temple keep.

Into a rock infused

They would have you believe
that a king is made when upon him a crown is laid,
but it is not so.

They would have you see
that a mitre makes a man mightier,
but it is not so.

They would have you accept
that a sceptre is so endowed it makes a man of power,
but it is not so.

It is not so for the rage will continue to flow.
It is not so for consuming self-hatred is not abated.
It is not so for unrelenting self-destruction is not mitigated.

So these rituals of investiture are to us delude,
keeping us securely occluded, into a rock infused.
Such are the customs of man in which we must stand.

By insisting from this downward culture a separation,
by Promethean labouring and unwavering dedication,
we may escape, and happy reach our high station.

For, behold,
the Kingdom of God
is within you.

Luke 17:21

In the Garden of the Night

In the Garden of the Night
by the moon's ghostly glow
let us walk the raked rows
that suddenly end.

They make me to suffocate.
I would escape.
Anything but this fate.

I wrestle with dragons
the best I can
but nothing alters this man's end.

Among corpses I did sit
and never felt this hard bit
that these rows suddenly ending
heave at me unrelenting.

O hand that in these rows placed
that which cannot be erased
I am by you released from the race.

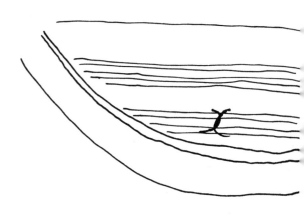

Spectacularly tossed

When an easy traveller, I did see
everywhere, fields fenced and hoed,
everywhere, homes of sand and gold,
everywhere, man timid and scolded.

Much was there marvellous:
everywhere, bridges and silos,
everywhere, motions and notions,
everywhere, restless commotions.

Then I was young and new,
nothing could I keep secure.
A mouse would an elephant become,
and them pacific, an army prolific.

Such was my lot, spectacularly tossed.
Now, when I travel, I am certain
of them past the fully drawn curtain.
I no more compromise with them I despise.

And in the cascade of valleys and hills,
only sheep do I see, from rim to rim.

In the world you shall have tribulations;
but be of good cheer,
I have overcome the world.
                    John 16:33

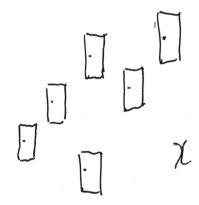

Embrace him given

Let me a little tell of giant battle,
when armies of strife unleash and fight
with countless rifles, missiles and flights.
They perform a million variations of aim and fire,
destroying that which the enemy did desire.

Similarly when war with the prince is waged,
him who battles as he has in every age,
unleashes his arsenal of mighty rage
in a million variations of aim and fire,
destroying that which the enemy did desire.

We are given no choice but to battle
this prince who by no rules is saddled.
It is doubtful you will any of this believe,
such is the camouflage that deceives.

I'll not be silent, though I speak in vain -
his artillery will never cease to rain
until you, mere human, embrace him given,
and in glorious war, be no more driven.

To him that overcometh
will I give to eat
of the tree of life,
which is in the midst of paradise.
Revelations 2:7

From him I away turn

Tell me friend
where I am to go to see forever.
Am I to sit on the rim of the earth
my feet dangling over a pool of a million stars
to see forever?
You are silent, friend.
By this do you imply forever is nearby?
Let me look then on my fellow man
who plays out his time underneath a thin tin veneer
of pretended happiness.
Let me look upon his steely face
always peeking, seeking advantage.
At once I am relieved
for here I see forever.
Forever he is lost
forever on the storm he's tossed
forever him I'll spurn
forever away I'll turn.

Tiger, go away

Yesterday while walking, easily contemplating
in my forest tall and green,
a fierce tiger appeared from the unseen,
and in an instant, no more,
my collected peace stormed out the door.

This is what happens when white-water rafting
or sitting nicely colourful media imbibing.
All of our good is washed away
that we may confront the storm of the day.

Many things so loud or of science
grab us ferociously by the ear
as the tiger approaching near.

Upon this crisis to crisis we feed,
our constant hunger never remedied.
Then when convulsed and churning,
we are duped into morbidly discerning.

Poor me, I rally against the wind.
I should instead say, "Tiger, go away,
this is my forest, this is my day."

For the evildoers shall be
cut off
but those that wait upon the Lord,
they shall inherit the earth.
                    Psalm 37:9

This is the justice

It is not seemly or propitious how I trade
diamonds hard found for coals which abound,
palaces grandly bent for a one-man tent,
the mountain view rare for the bottom of a stair.

Then I am displeased and howl.
Once more I begin to uncover
only to trade as no other
in this cycle ruling my hour.

Like a sheep in a prairie pasture
I have found more than I could gather,
and according to my master
frantic, coal is surely better.

This is the justice before me unfolding,
for in the weak there is only the burning.

Therefore hell hath enlarged herself
and opened her mouth without measure.
Isaiah 5:14

Such a surprise, Paradise

The still, small voice

This is the beginning -
here in this vast James Bay
in its bounty of water and endless summer day
the Lord upon this land made man.
No! Not yesterday or in past ages
but today made he one of his sages.

This is my beginning
which like the petals of a rose
unfurls, forever unfolds.
Gently I feel my limbs anew
open in the loving kindness
flowing in my heart.
Now I could embrace the end of the race
for with new choice
came the still, small voice.

Now I steer

Moses in a bark of reeds
was by caring hands
placed upon the water.
By nurturing hands I too was sent to sea.
My little bark was frail,
there was no way to steer.
This was my lot for many a year.
These were the days without a true teacher.

When this skiff I did outgrow
I joined with the dolphins
and lived in the sea, simply.
Later came the Shark who set me apart
from the easy company.
Teeth ripped and did tear -
there seemed no end of him.
He stayed hard upon me,
this beast of my dismembering.

Then one day on the sea tossing
old crates I assembled
into a very seaworthy craft.
This is now a ship of steel
which I humbly steer.

A glorious high throne

When you were a little child
your daddy would sit you on his knee
and give you a great bear hug.
Your arms tried mightily
but could reach only his big sides.
Your daddy told you stories,
and woke up your dreams.
I watched him in love with you,
tired and worn from labouring in the cold of men's hearts.

Many a time he'd say, "You are bound for glory."
Then he'd change it into something else.
He said it so often with so much hope for you,
that I got caught up, and began to believe.
Believe that you were special.
Believe that your destiny was a high throne,
and that there you would find peace.

Now that you've grown, it's marvellous to see
how your daddy's saying has come true,
for you have reached a glorious high throne,
which from the BEGINNING,
is the only place of our SANCTUARY.

A glorious high throne
from the beginning
is the place of our sanctuary.
                    Jeremiah 17:12

Escape his gutting horn

Hey, listen up, if Zeus got mad, when he was top dog
in the Hellenic pantheon, he didn't run to the bottle
nor to Cronus and Rhea, his father and mother.
Instead he stretched forth from Olympus
and hurled down on Poseidon and Hades
all of the force
of his lightning and thunder.

Now I am angry, I stand, I unleash
upon mine enemy the same
that I silence him in the storm
and escape his gutting horn.

Please yourself

O Child of my living life, my living heart,
I am a heathen, savaged, daily taken apart.
Yet, living life, peace of my fine art,
let not the screams hailing, us part.

O Child, my living heart, my eyes I shut
(which are so very tired of seeing sluts)
that I may glimpse you and plead,
please yourself, but enter me and lead.

O Child of my living life, glory on earth,
I need you as a ship needs a berth.
I need you as a kite needs flight.
Come, noble one, and be my living life.

Let not my past failings you deter
but rise and make of me the living pure.

O Lord God, be clothed
with salvation
and let thy saints
rejoice in goodness.
                    II Chronicles 6:41

Our share of kindness

There shall be an end
an end of his rule
over me.

Certainly these torments that
chain the child
to dreadful beatings upon beatings
will have an end.

Surely too there shall be an end of these
gruesome
forever shadows
he, mine ruler, installs high and higher over me in the
criminal inversion that fills me with despair.

Then will my child be
free
to make an end of his rule
and still the frenzied dance
of these reflections I abhor,
that finally we may have
our share of kindness.

Gladly come

I am thy Living Life,
thy progress in the New Land.
I am given to thee
that ye have liberty.

I am thy transformation
from perdition to salvation,
from war to peace,
from death to life.

I am not as you of flesh and blood.
I am as these others, beyond natural.
I am a might, a power unimaginable.
I am he who will not flee.

I am thy light in this long night.
I am all of thy good and more.
I am too in need of thee;
gladly come, walk with me.

In that day sing unto her,
A vineyard of red wine.
                    Isaiah 27:2

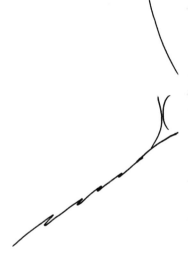

Conquered by the thief

Yesterday by twilight
I was gaily rounding the perimeter
of the Canadian National Railway Tower.
I could see countless men in the streets -
O how they used to maim me,
these endless lame.
It has been ages between hearing
King
Queen
and knowing their emptiness.
Now that I am no longer fed by grief
let them fall away, let them fall,
them conquered by the thief.

So very glad

Here I am, my grand Lord -
I had not expected arriving
for the master of fictions
had me firmly in his domain.
I had given up, thought lost,
so sure were his chains.

And the mortuary heightened despair.
I expected knowing only torments,
for he had invaded and decimated.

Yet here I am, my high Lord,
humble and full of awe,
after the long time of no believing,
after the long time of all denying.

Such a relief to no more be drowned.
So very glad, I touch thy hand.

For my righteousness
the Lord hath brought me in
to possess this land.
                    Deuteronomy 9:4

In the vernacular

Friend
you order me
to be constant
in the storm
to guard the newborn
unto death
to keep my feet
on yours.
These I do and I receive
my release from the abyss
which in the vernacular we call
peace.

There is no higher

It does seem as with Jason who was goaded by King Pelias
that I too am compelled to assemble and then pass by
that mighty dragon which does not sleep
in search of one thread from the Golden Fleece.

Now before me on this walk of old appears a line of gold
woven by a few fine hands into a rope bold.
They who lower it from above
are my brothers who from this abyss have moved on.

I cannot tell of this place so very hard
for much must one do to enter
and then avoid becoming paralyzed.
As well eyes set on purest gold
must be bolstered to escape their close.

Climbing out I precisely thread my new strand
from the Golden Fleece into this high line
that someday will be as mighty as that
holding the Golden Gate span which takes us to land.

Happy am I of this golden line
as the argonauts on Colchis in their time.
This my brothers did skilfully build
to assist them of open will,
to rise and reach to where there is no higher.

The West Wind. 1917
Tom Thomson

You are truly as me

I see from the tatami-covered veranda
of my temple
how the sliding panes
frame a panorama
of pines and maples captured
in the magic of the light.
I am proud of this perfection.
Who did build this beauty bold?
Who could tell of this serenity?
I am raised into myself
in a kindness.
I give thee praise, framers of Daitoku-ji,
for you are truly as me.
You cast to still the ravenings
that sweep away my generation.

Dare part the curtain

My good friend travelling this road
of eternal mystery, heavily loaded,
you'll rightly ask and deserve to know
who else does this hard way go.

None are here! I speak without tears:
Not them adorned by cathedral spires.
Not them adorned by ivory towers.
Not them adorned by executive powers.

So rest well, my friend kind;
feel a perfect ease, thy heart to please.
I stand ever so certain
that only we, dare part the curtain.

And thou son of man, be not afraid of them
neither be afraid of their words
though briers and thorns be with thee.
                              Ezekiel 2:6

In an ageless way

In the silence of the desert,
under endless stars
I praise this day
for the child is raised
to judge.

He has closed the gate
where the blind rage.
In the transformation he abides
free
in the new land of mystery
in a power greater than the prince's.

Hands once paralyzed now unlock.
This I say in an ageless way.
I mark the place
that this road all might trace.

By your grace

Joy to me is your rising living life,
out from the haze of miserable strife.
Bounty and wonder of man complete,
the promise of no more defeat.

Do not anymore go away,
enter me more and here stay.
Without you I am forlorn,
dying in the master's storm.

The ocean boundless I would corral,
the clouds gathering I would dispel,
for my deep desire is to have you near,
only your judgement do I long to hear.

And when the master seeks to return
by your grace we'll him spurn.

Would God that all the Lord's people
were prophets.

Numbers 11:29

To labour sweetly

Ah but to labour sweetly,
to sweat in joy,
not as a wind-up toy.

Grand it is to labour sweetly
and reach that exhaustion of peace
which he dare not transgress.

The bounty of love

I was born a clam
And did clam things,
Also sex.
How else clams?
This I was until I became a man,
Past the muscle stage,
Past that dramatic, perplexing place
Where there is not a moment calm.
Constantly does the sea alarm.
This I was until I became an angel
Soaring like a fluffy cloud,
Seeing the sea below and further down
Full of man and yappy clams.
I am the serenity blue
In the bounty of love
Radiating from above.

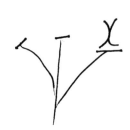

For we wrestle
not against flesh and blood
but against principalities.

Ephesians 6:12

Freedom

In the promised land of my salvation
between Great Slave Lake and Athabasca
I have from trade won release
and more for I now have peace -
far more, for judgement I now hear
in this vast space of caribou and deer.

The other inhabitants full of doubts rage.
Everything they deny, their custom of ages.
Always they lie and besmirch,
eyes locked on bountiful earth.

Here, I no more fear the night,
the storm awakening or any blight.
In this promised land glorious
I am free to make happy choices.

I am come down to deliver them
to bring them unto a good land and large,
unto a land flowing with milk and honey.
                                    Exodus 3:8

Wind-swept clouds

Sometimes I moan, O look at me -
all my efforts nothing show,
well past youth's new glow.
Has the temple within
fallen to some sin
or does it stand,
the pride of the land?
Out I go to ask again.

Little heifer born pride of cattle,
long ago when I was twenty-seven
you with those large eyes looked my way
then turned calmly to a bale of golden hay.
Today my hair is a soft grey,
much have I decided without delay.
Will the temple shed the storm?
You snort and into the field cavort.

Little one born in this field of green,
you and I have business to be seen.
But henceforth the fault is mine
when in you I seek a mirror.
All of the steps I've climbed
are to you wind-swept clouds.

Judgement's end

This day Bacchus surrounded by nymphs and satyrs
sways the crowd to madness and bubbles.
In a mad frenzy of wine and beer
they conceal sadness out of dreadful fear.

This day too your brothers left the dying -
be as them and live on Mount Zion.
Their eyes in the Transformation unsealed,
O be as them and forever be healed.

In us your living life, rise and raise.
In us your living life, love and be loved.
In us your living life, feel, flow in grace.

In me living life, hear judgement's end.
In me living life, become peace on earth.
In me living life, be raised from the dead.

Is it time for you,
O ye, to dwell in your cieled house,
and this house lie waste?
Haggai 1:4

Freedom reached

I have reached the Promised Land
albeit only the shore.
Here I stand a free man
emancipated from the roar.

In my freedom I am seeing,
I am purely feeling
every fibre of myself awake.
Now let time and circumstance
enter my unshakeable embrace.

I am free to look upon the lion tamed,
to stroke with pleasure his supple mane.
I keep a sure hold on this tress
to make an end of repining restlessness.

Now I call out to you,
freedom reached
is all I can do.

I take what is mine

I am the life risen
out of Hecate's prison.
Out of night and darkness
was I born in harness
to rise past ghosts and shades,
past gloomy and horrible places.

On forlorn days and sunny,
valleys deep or mountains climbing,
I shall keep here
in every coming year.

When the master is harsh
in sorrow I march.
When from him I am shielded
joy flows unimpeded.

Let not the master ruling
stone us into confusion.
Let come the day
his rule is put away
and I take what is mine
to hold to the end of time.

Verily I say unto you,
Except ye become as little children,
ye shall not enter the kingdom.
                              Matthew 18:3

From Ryoan-ji I'll not part

Across the span of several thousand years
I bow to you my friend to me near.
In this twenty-first century Ryoan-ji rests
just as your hand each pebble set.
Your eye had a rare might.
You did know by the inner sight.
I see the same interplay
of men and endless caverns
from this Lake Ontario shore today.

When I behold what you did build
I am proud of your pure will.
By the boldness of your power
men may cease today to cower.
With mighty courage and high dignity
you realized the eternal temple mystery
which with my eye free I am able to see.
I am so very pleased with thee.

I am happy for your hour
as mine ticks away.
I stand certain in your great discernment.
I keep you in my heart,
from Ryoan-ji I'll not part.

Grace and light

Without thee,
glorious, grand and potent being
given to me,
I would lie here decimated.

Without thee,
life, love, in judgement secure,
rising pure,
I would lie here to all inured.

Without thee,
grace and light of awesome might,
entering to rule,
I would lie here sad and cruel.

Verily I say unto you,
Whosoever shall not receive
the kingdom of God as a little child,
he shall not enter therein.
                              Mark 10:15

Life in a new world

Majestic light, grace on earth, my saving hand,
let me embrace you in this barbaric land.
Barbarians spurn you for they cannot love,
they reject you for they are full of harm.
Barbarians of sorrow know no tomorrow,
they are a wasting, flooded by horrors.

Majestic light, my living grace and glory,
I am awed, I marvel at your presence joyous.
No coronation or investment could be so grand
as your rising in me in this sad land.

You are my living life in a new world,
my transformation out of them sold.
You are the beginning of my discernment,
the end of the perpetual internment.

Behold now Behemoth,
which I made with thee;
he eateth grass as an ox.

Job 40:15

In these places that we meet

A fellow traveller Augustine upon me urged,
"There is a place of quiet not to be disturbed."
This I did not understand, nor did I tell;
like the brand on a cow I kept it well.

It would have been better, raising the matter,
but sadly, teachers here are widely scattered.
In my incomprehension the line I did not neglect,
but from time to time on it I would reflect.

Years later when the roar of the flames was quelled,
this line came fully alive like a bell
for I had reached the place of quiet
at the interstices of God's power.

Now my breath I hold for great is my desire to tell
though it is almost impossible describing the steps out of hell.

Like a man chained to an unexploded bomb
I keep the quiet undisturbed avoiding any wrong.
With all of my being I labour to stop the igniting -
this is my feeling in this place exciting.

I tremble in fear for it is so trying
stopping this giant from rising.
I am like one kneeling, whose will is keeping
the guillotine from releasing.

I am awed by the powers herein collected.
I am awed by the way secret and perilous.
Like the pilot whose engines have died
I do what I must to keep flying.

In these places that we meet, myself
I keep, in loving-kindness
and him certainly quiet.

When victory is ours

I swear with all of my being
never to abandon you
my friend in the war.

Though fear and worries pound in my head
I will not abandon you
my friend in the war.

Though the enemy is larger than Vesuvius
and I am as a reed
I shall abide by you my friend.

Though deafening the roaring, brutal the storming
and I am as a sigh
I shall abide by you my friend.

Though the battle relentless is as a flood
and I am as a pebble
I shall abide by you my friend.

And when the victory is ours,
I a mere human and you from Paradise
shall abide in joy.

For with thee is the fountain of life:
in thy light shall we see light.
Psalm 36:9

Low as a snail

Let me in every thing fail
let me stay low as a snail
let me be unseen and unheard
let me not any man disturb.

But grant me what can be mine,
to him tether and quiet,
then in the peace of a child
I'll proudly abide.

Drowned Land, Algoma. *1918*
Franklin Carmichael

What must be seen and not read

Gentle friend come here and see -
I know it's not the temple of Apollo at Delphi.
It is a pond pool straightforward
not the shrine of the Pythian oracle.
It is surrounded by trees and grasses
not the broad slopes of Parnassus.
Yet it is a scene unblemished
with gray mist in green pines dancing
and the quivering still reflection
is a rare moment of perfection.
Its form and motion pure and complete
does outdo the Gulf of Corinth,
and henceforth I'll not tread
on what must be seen and not read.

How I've travelled

If only I'd been sold a map
I might have avoided the trap.
If only I'd seen a model of this place
I wouldn't have searched in outer space.
If only I'd been something taught
I wouldn't have been easily caught.

How deep the swamp I couldn't tell -
it turned out a bottomless well.
And the rocks there you'd think were sure
but they rose full of desires impure.
There was not a voice kind and clear,
no man I saw not ruled by fear.

How I've travelled is truly wondrous,
proof we can rise above the ponderous.
I long to reach you out there seeking,
searching in bins, everywhere peeking.
There is one thing I'd like to say:
let nothing keep you at bay.

For loving-kindness can be yours in peace,
despite the errors and the noise that never cease.

There is nothing from without a man
that entering into him can defile him;
but the things which come out of him,
those are they that can defile the man.
                            Mark 7:15

A new passage

I have no desire to say anything about man,
media, or business where towers stand.
No desire to speak about that which is seen,
science, or the sad culture on the screen.

I seek only in myself to travel, surely unravel
these iron mysteries with which I am saddled.
This is my longing, my only quest -
to this I give my life and escape the rest.

In the transformation I did rise spectacular
through Aetna to Olympus on the Adriatic.
I did escape long incarceration on Alcatraz
to a rare and fine liberty, first of the class.

I rose out of self-destruction and self-hatred
to loving-kindness and am no more naked.
I rose out of battles unending and full of ravages
to the river Eunoe with shields, a new passage.

So many strands I needed to knit,
the number staggering, so hard the fit;
but now the war and its tallies
give way to peace and calm sallies.

For he put on righteousness as a breastplate,
and a helmet of salvation upon his head,
and he put on the garments of vengeance for clothing,
and was clad with zeal as a cloak.
                    Isaiah 59:17

I am writing to confess

My friend I am writing to confess
that I am feeling mystified.
Upon The New Land I have arrived.

But much to my surprise
I find no greeting or happy meeting.
Is this not revealing?

Countless events have their acknowledgement
but on the shore of The New Land
the stillness I hear is disquieting.

Can I speak of this to the deaf, show the blind
or tell them who ought to know?
It would be like eating only snow.

My friend, you who travelled here before
know well this sandy shore.
I happily follow, seeking nothing more.

But forgive me one sigh,
for the many outside
who this beach will not reach.

My friend I must not digress.
I leave the tumbling sea behind
and in pure joy abide.

I am your brother

No one sees my home in plain view
where I am naked and out of ruses,
so for those out there able to care,
I'll describe my house in the rare air.

It is the good place solid and sound,
furnished nicely and light abounds.
It has just one little oddity -
it has no walls, not even the halls.

Getting by in here is a spectacular sight
for in comes the day, in comes the night.
The wind enters in every season
to heave and tatter with no reason.

Now if ever you discover
yourself, in a place as no other,
do not your nakedness cover -
remember me, I am your brother.

He that believeth not the Son
shall not see life;
but the wrath of God
abideth in him.
                    John 3:36

The diamond to be seen

Deep in the centre at the side of the temple
in joy I glance at the bamboo there planted
revealing that which is impossible to tell.

I look at the leaves proliferating and jump in joy -
no, not as a sweet little boy
but a man full-aged in the war.

In this tiny grove is a mighty ploy
whose secret unravelled fills me with joy.
It truly is magical, this bamboo haphazard.

Somehow I glean the diamond to be seen
and at one with its creator complete the dream.

Cages everywhere

My good Lord, my living life in the promised land:
Why am I so alone every day at work and at play?
Men talk of sons and success, of family and place,
while I keep silent for I have no place in the race.

Yet - I do not lament or decry
for I have escaped the claws of lies.
Yet - I do not of my loneliness despair
for I see their cages everywhere.

I have played them as a cat with clear intention
doing with a mouse what I shall not mention.
In times past I sought them out for their charm
and came away saddened, feeling only harm.

I am alone, this I accept, alone I stand
if ever I am to escape from this sand.
This is my lot past man's subterfuge
for family and position are a destroying deluge.

I stand alone before endless fields of grazers.
I stand alone before You, living life of ages,
and steadfast in this judgement of men
our unity forms and loneliness has an end.

I am the Lord which exercises
loving-kindness, judgement, and righteousness
in the earth:
for in these things I delight.
                    Jeremiah 9:24

147

The end of night

Living life full of grace,
love upon earth,
beauty upon man,
light upon darkness.

Living life, man's transformation,
the sea is calmed,
the earth is tamed,
we walk no more lame.

Living life, man's only strength,
we keep thee,
we heed thee.
In thy might ends the night.

Living life, potent tower,
happy are we in thy power.

Behold
the Lamb of God
which taketh away
the sin of the world.
                              John 1:29

Majestic and potent

O so quiet, still and delicate,
nothing like when men gather.
O the moment of dawn,
you are steady and calm.

O so secure, not hurried
or rabid, grace thy habit.
To them you are so illusive
that He sacrificed to prove you.

O so high and wide,
a giant on every side.
You see all in a peek,
and return it formed and complete.

O so majestic and potent,
forming a perfect moment.
To all you offer a warm embrace
for in you is no doubt of their place.

You plant steel where once was straw,
delicate grace, out of rock water you draw.

I considered all of the living
which walk under the sun,
with the second child
that shall stand up in his stead.
                              Ecclesiastes 4:15

Shoreline. *1936*
Emily Carr

I have found my station

Friend of my heart I write to you
from our narrow road to tell that the great load
which I had to carry is now light as a fairy.

You used to remind me in many ways
that the interplay of sun and sky
and the endless swirling of clouds and streams
gave to each of us a feeling so special,
of having a place, not just in the race,
of being a full part of the greater art.
It is these delicate hues, these aqua blues,
that let us have a hand in that which is grand.

My friend who made me certain of the beauty ringing potent,
I confess that which was shattered now is gathered
and in this flowing creation I have found my station.

Loving-one majestic

Living Life, my soul redeeming,
grand and glorious is thy seeing.
You are the flower of my believing,
the hope of man past the dreaming.

Tell me, loving-one majestic,
about all of these so tragic -
what can to them be made sensible
that they no more fear and tremble.

Revealing me is your soldierly duty
to them scattered in the cowardly mutiny;
all that is possible must be done
that they understand and no more run.

None see me and this is no surprise
though I am their life, their eyes.
You must not rest until they rise
or they shall pass knowing only lies.

The stake is life or death in the war you wage,
for men are today as in the stone age.
So, poet noble, do all to lift
for endless are them down in the pit.

He brought me up
out of a horrible pit,
out of the miry clay,
and set my feet on rock.

                    Psalm 40:2

Beginning of time

Before thee I confess
you are my peace,
my soul redeemed.

Before thee I am full of awe
for I speak, and boldly.
In past days I was ever defeated
and brutally savaged
in the war.

Before thee I confess that without thee
I would forever be defeated, forever savaged.

Before thee I am full of awe -
for now begins time
and ends dying.

Blessed are the meek
for they shall inherit the earth.
Matthew 5:5

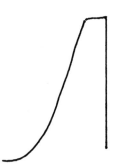

Beguiled beast

Some of us have been set free
from the trappings, from the machinery
by which careerists and fashioneestes are charmed,
not one little bit suspecting their harm.

Some of us have gone on to greater station
than those noises politicking in the nation,
than those by club and tribe measuring -
all manner of illusion treasuring.

Some of us unseen pass before eyes
though to the inward one we materialize.
With friends and peers we are as before
despite the fact that we are not there any more.

For we are them released
from the easily fooled beast.

For they have sown the wind
and they shall reap the whirlwind.
                                    Hosea 8:7

This I vow to do

If day and night I strove for light
getting nearer to the living-life,
I would be at peace.

If I felt sure of the lot of them
that falter and thereafter descend,
I would be at peace.

If loving-kindness flowed in this man
I'd be a part of the grand plan.
I would be at peace.

If I were sure of the work of my hand
with my true brothers I'd stand.
I would be at peace.

But mine enemy is before me.
By his poisons I am taken
and my peace is shaken.

On this road him I must pass
and this I vow to do
for another round or two.

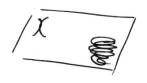

But his delight is in the law of the Lord;
and in his law doth he meditate
day and night.
                                    Psalm 1:2

Our house fantastic

In my new house so rare,
reached by a very treacherous stair,
I am shielded and sure,
for all is constant and secure.

My new home is great and grand,
a place rare upon this land.
Many would such a dwelling build,
but too easily do they lose will.

Self-hatred here is no more;
it cannot pass inside the door.
Every other house it does dominate -
such is the present landscape.

With open arms all are received,
for here we cannot be deceived.
Yet few dare to arrive,
so hard it is to strive.

Such is our house fantastic -
nothing is there more majestic.

And Jesus went into
the temple of God,
and cast out all of them that sold and bought
in the temple.
                              Matthew 21:12

A mirror unbroken

All my days I've laboured
in high and low places
looking for a mirror unbroken.

No school, no steeple bell,
nothing made by man's hand
did my self reflect.

Such was my lot. Believe.
Never a sure sign or a friend.
Finally I set about
making stone steps
on which I could depend,
for nothing unsure
nothing impure
will here endure.

Now clear signs
pointing the climb
are securely placed
for all who alone
must seek a way home.